Laurent La Gamba

A Contribution to American Art History

26 revisited works from the Whitney Museum

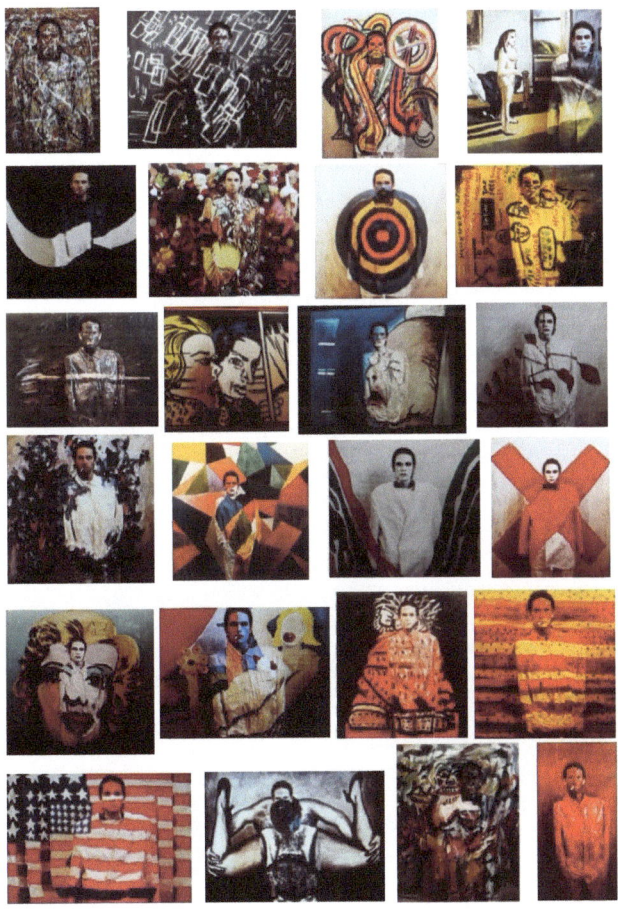

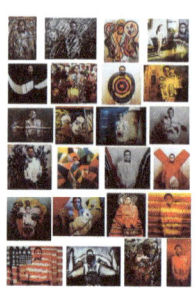

Laurent La Gamba
A Contribution to American Art History,
26 revisited works from the Whitney Museum.
Copyright © Laurent La Gamba, 2014

ISBN: 9781500568290

Printed in the United States of America

Cover: Laurent La Gamba, **Self-portrait as Robert Mangold's** *Three Red X Within X*, 2002, acrylic on board and protective suit, color photograph, 75 x 50 cm. (Photo courtesy of and copyright Laurent La Gamba)

Matisse 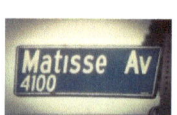 *Avenue Books*

Laurent La Gamba

A Contribution to American Art History,

26 revisited works from the Whitney Museum
(Preface by Lyn Cole)

The subject of this series is American art.

This project was carried out in March 2002 in the artist's studio in Monléon-Magnoac, France. The aim of the exercise was to revisit some famous American works of art, exhibited at the Whitney Museum of Art in New York, through the lens of the artist's very specific take on camouflage.

It is a studio piece in contrast to the artist's other series which were generally performances outside the studio.

Each piece has to be considered as a painting, an installation, a performance as well as a conceptual photograph.

Each photograph is an interpretation by the artist, a perfectly subjective appropriation of the work in hand. If the figure of the artist is central in this series too, it merely serves to emphasise the exceptional character of the original works.

Matisse 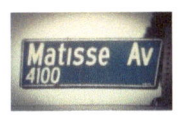 Avenue Books

For Eliot and Raphaël...

"N'en doute point, Socrate ! dit-elle. Car justement les hommes eux-mêmes, si sur leur ambition tu consens à porter ton regard, tu seras confondu de son absurdité; à moins que tu ne réfléchisses à ce que je t'ai dit et que tu ne médites sur l'étrange état où les met l'amour de la renommée, le désir de se ménager pour l'éternité du temps une gloire immortelle. Pour cette fin, ils sont prêts à courir tous les périls les plus périlleux, plus encore que pour leurs enfants, à dépenser leurs biens, à endurer de dures fatigues quelles qu'elles soient, à mourir pour l'atteindre ! "

Platon, Le banquet.

Preface

Laurent La Gamba's insertion of himself into American art history is an impudent gesture which could be regarded as immodest were it not for the selflessness he displays in paying homage to the series of iconic works he has selected.

The very specific use of camouflage and self-portraiture, defining characteristics of his own work, are put to good use in this revisiting of the American pantheon.

He blends himself into the American tradition via these two techniques which, far from imposing a reading upon these paintings, open up the possibilities of identification for the author. "I am another" takes on a whole new dimension.
The paintings themselves are merely sketched in as background to representations of himself, there is no attempt to do more than make the images identifiable and given their iconic status this is readily achieved.

The focus is upon the artist's engagement with the works selected, these choices are emblematic and allow the artist to lay claim to a certain allegiance with the various masculine ideals thus portrayed. Jim Dine's "Black Shovel" for example could exemplify an ironic distance from the American blue-collar worker known for his straight talking and his solidarity with his fellows; Jasper John's "Three Flags" on the other hand conveys a doubt about the excesses of American patriotism and where it might lead; de Kooning's Abstract Expressionist work along with Jackson Pollock's famous drip paintings are forever associated with macho self-destructiveness due to the artists' addiction to alcohol, while the Pop art of Lichtenstein speaks to the abolition of the distinction between high art and mass media and the expansion of the realm of the artist. Basquiat's graffiti art and its subsequent absorption into the canon as well as the recognition of Mapplethorpe's photographs as art are a demonstration of this shift. Warhol was of course acknowledged as the game-changer and no account of American art would be complete without him. La Gamba has selected his "Marilyn" to impose his own image upon thus opening up a Pandora's box of identifications. Not only is gender an issue but Warhol's use of the image of Marilyn Monroe confronts his own sexuality or lack thereof and confirms him in the role of voyeur. This has reverberations for La Gamba since he chooses to use camouflage as a way into this painting, he takes pleasure in luring the viewer into a contemplation of him as Warhol's "Marilyn", throwing into question sexual identity and assuming an identification with an artist who took delight in transvestism. We enter a veritable hall of mirrors with all of the distortions that that entails, this is surely the artist's intention.

La Gamba's facility in conjuring up the work of other artists is matched by his simultaneous assertion and annihilation of self through the process of camouflage. He both wants and does not want to be seen. He uses the self-portrait as a way of usurping an artist's work while laying claim to it whilst camouflage allows him to disappear into a work he is also laying claim to; both practices manifest respect. This is a tradition in art, you have to acknowledge your masters, or mistresses for that matter. It appears that the desire to be seen or not seen is evenly balanced since approximately half of these works involve camouflage and the other half more conscious self-portraiture. The self portraits tend to emphasise the instability of identity while camouflage implies the evaporation of identity altogether. The artist is playing with notions of slippage, of the recognition of an absence of identity and of the need to cling to some fictive support to enable us to engage with the world. We are summoned to witness his multiple selves as they parade before us in the guise of Jackson Pollock, Philip Guston, Cy Twombly, Andy Warhol et al and it serves to clarify what we mean by claiming an identity, even a false one, since, at some level, all identities are constructs.

Take La Gamba's use of the cigarette as a trope, it is deliberately misleading, he does not smoke, yet the viewer makes assumptions about his character from this lone signifier. He is toying with our prejudices.

The ludic quality of La Gamba's involvement with his work draws the viewer in and obliges him/her to reflect on his/her own status in relation to these "masterpieces" of American art.

This is the only vanishing act which draws attention to itself. The artist derives pleasure from disconcerting his audience and, curiously enough, the audience derives pleasure from this deliberate attempt to confuse it. We enjoy being bamboozled by a profusion of selves portrayed in the context of American Modern Art which both mislead and entice the viewer into La Gamba's self-professed identifications, none of which have any ultimate hold upon us or the artist.

Lyn Cole

Laurent La Gamba

A Contribution to American Art History,

26 revisited works from the Whitney Museum

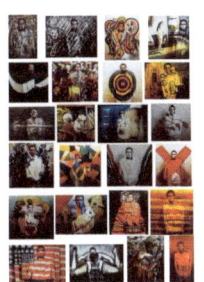

Self-portrait as a Jackson Pollock painting, 2002 Procryptic painting (acrylic on board and protective suit) color photograph, 75 x 50 cm

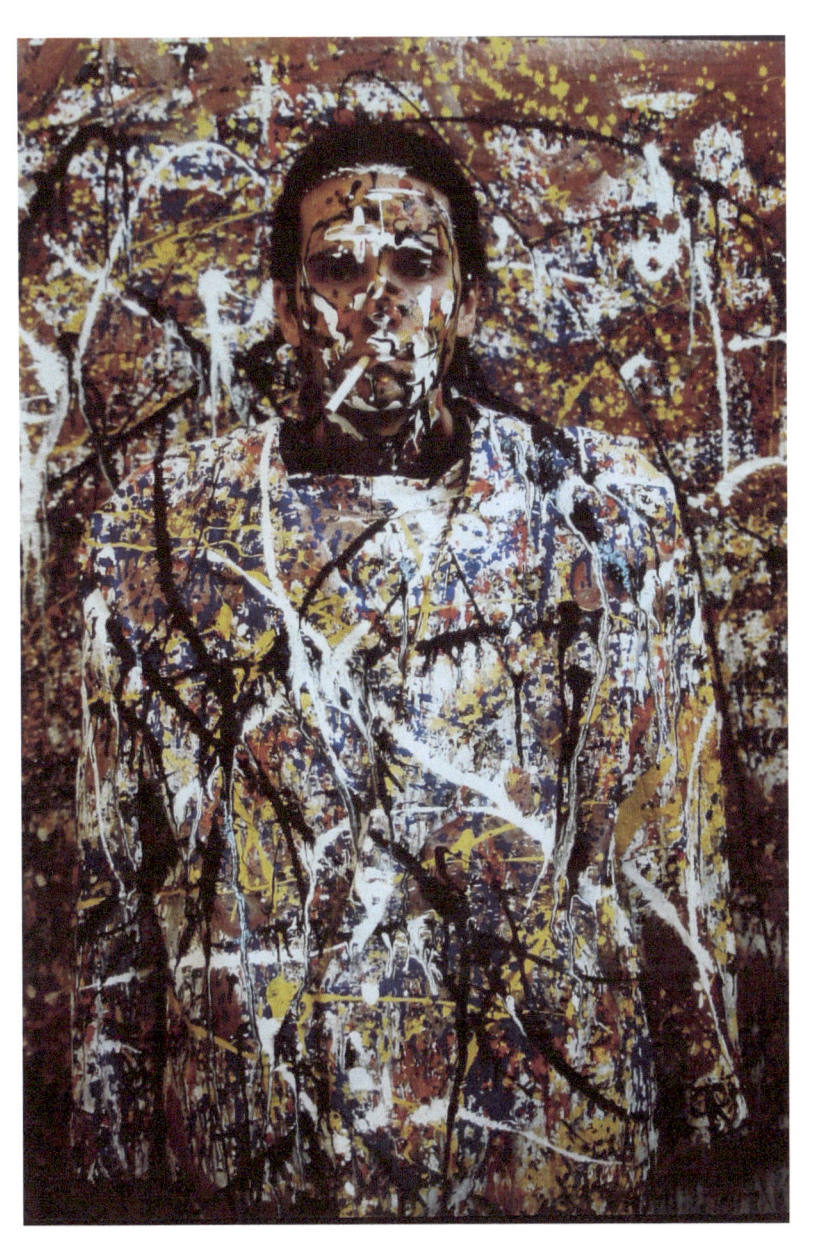

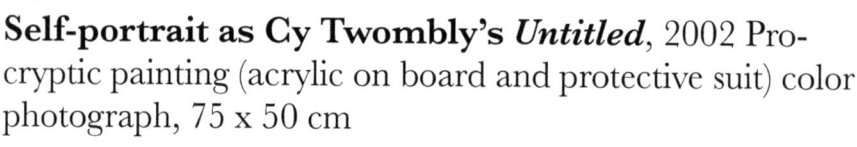

Self-portrait as Cy Twombly's *Untitled*, 2002 Procryptic painting (acrylic on board and protective suit) color photograph, 75 x 50 cm

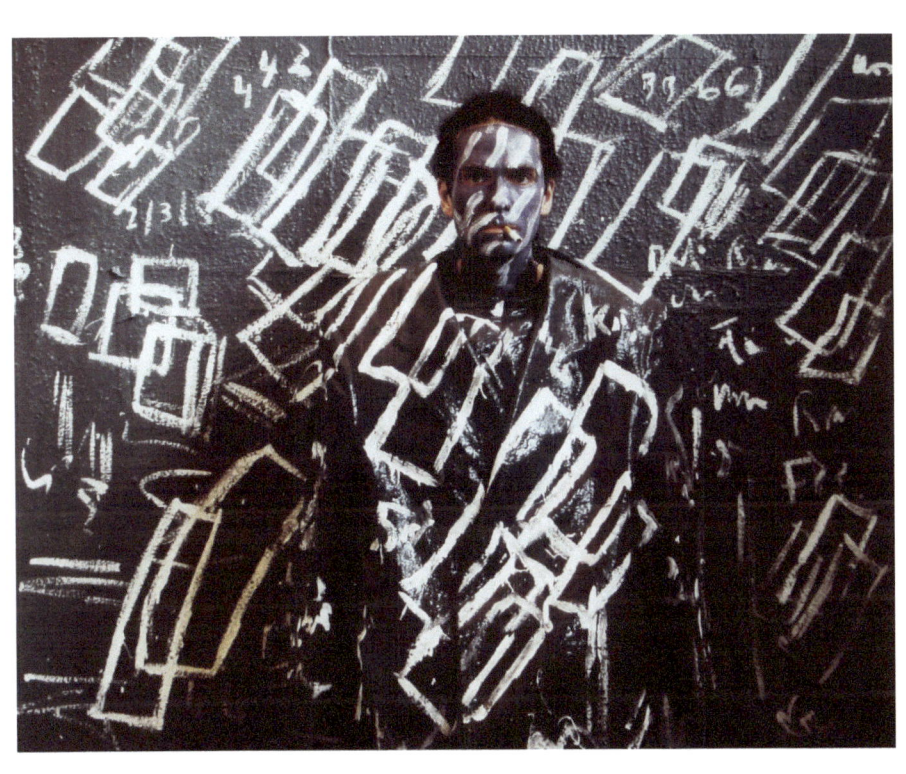

Self-portrait as Frank Stella's *Kastura*, 2002 Procryptic painting (acrylic on board and protective suit) color photograph, 75 x 50 cm

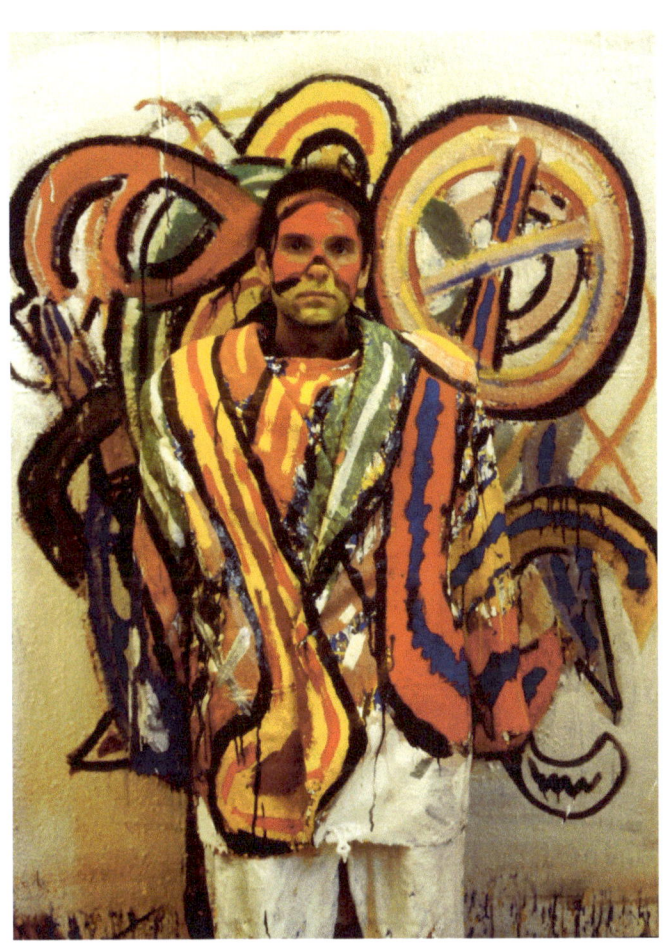

Self-portrait as Edward Hopper ´s *A woman in the sun*, 2002 Pro-cryptic painting (acrylic on board and protective suit) color photograph, 75 x 50 cm

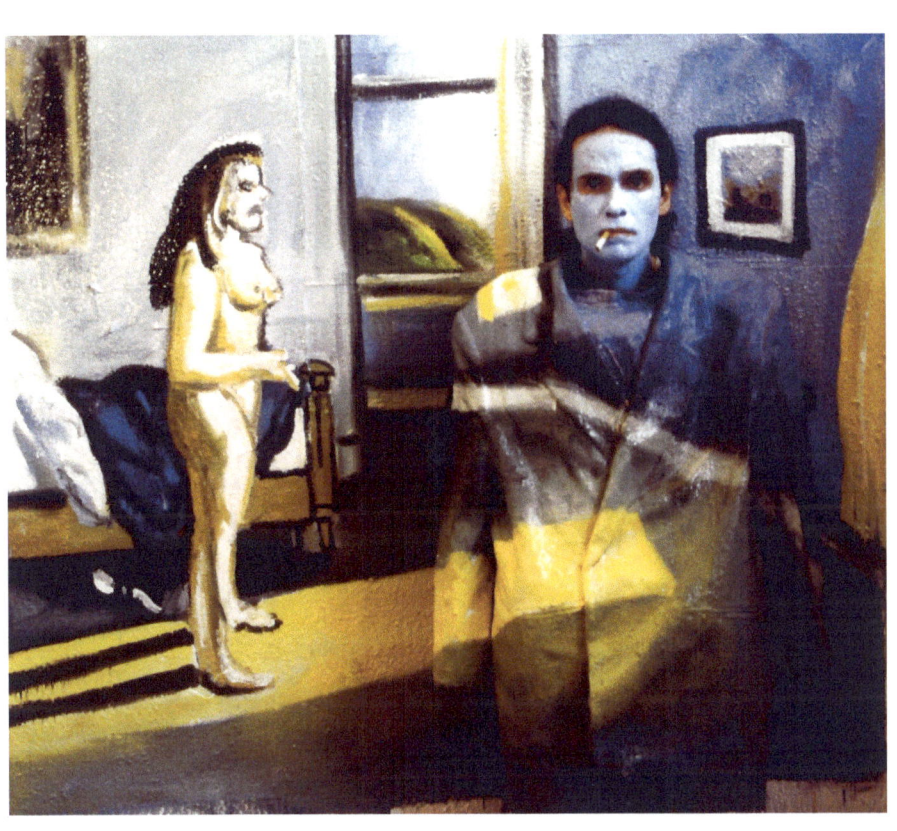

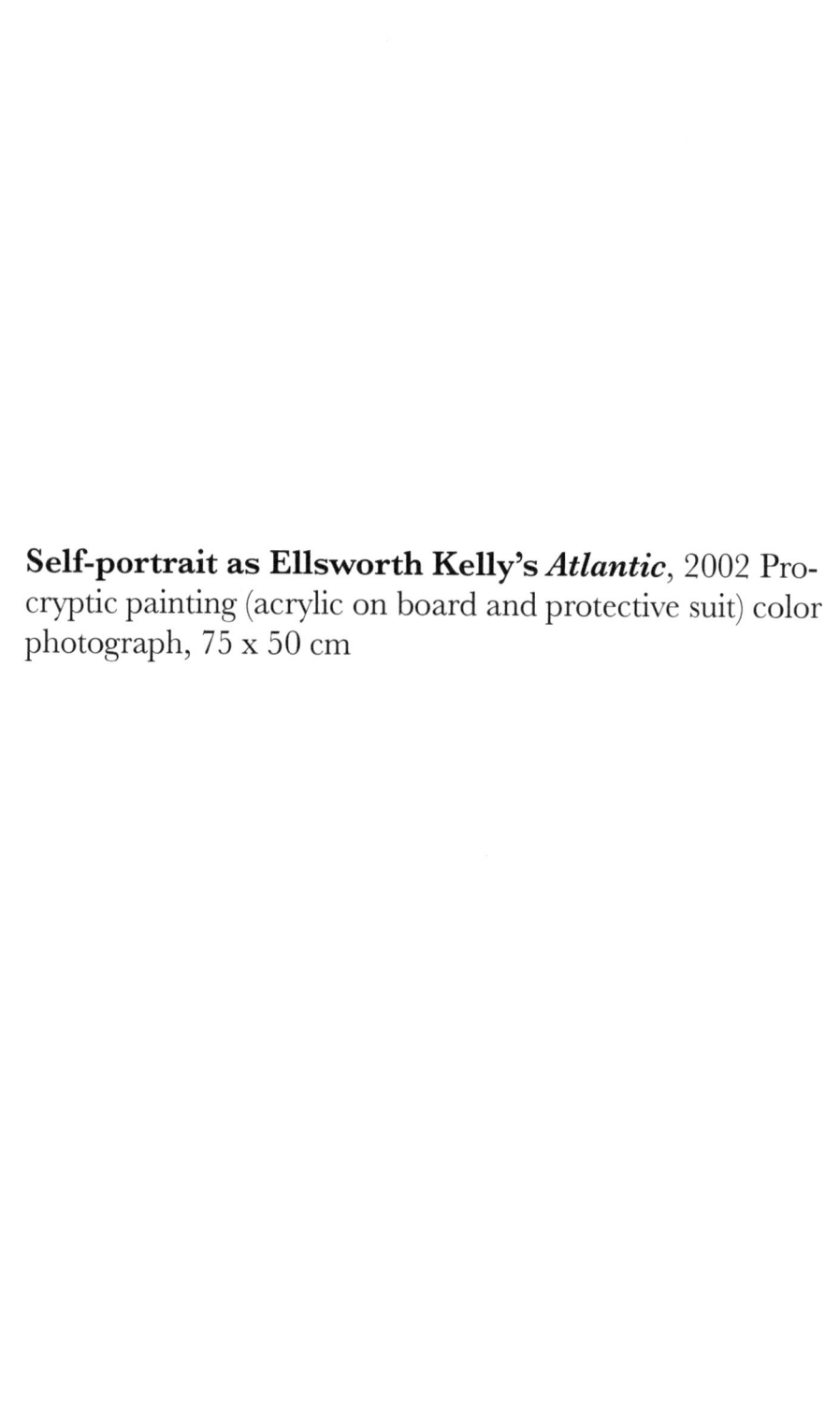

Self-portrait as Ellsworth Kelly's *Atlantic*, 2002 Pro-
cryptic painting (acrylic on board and protective suit) color
photograph, 75 x 50 cm

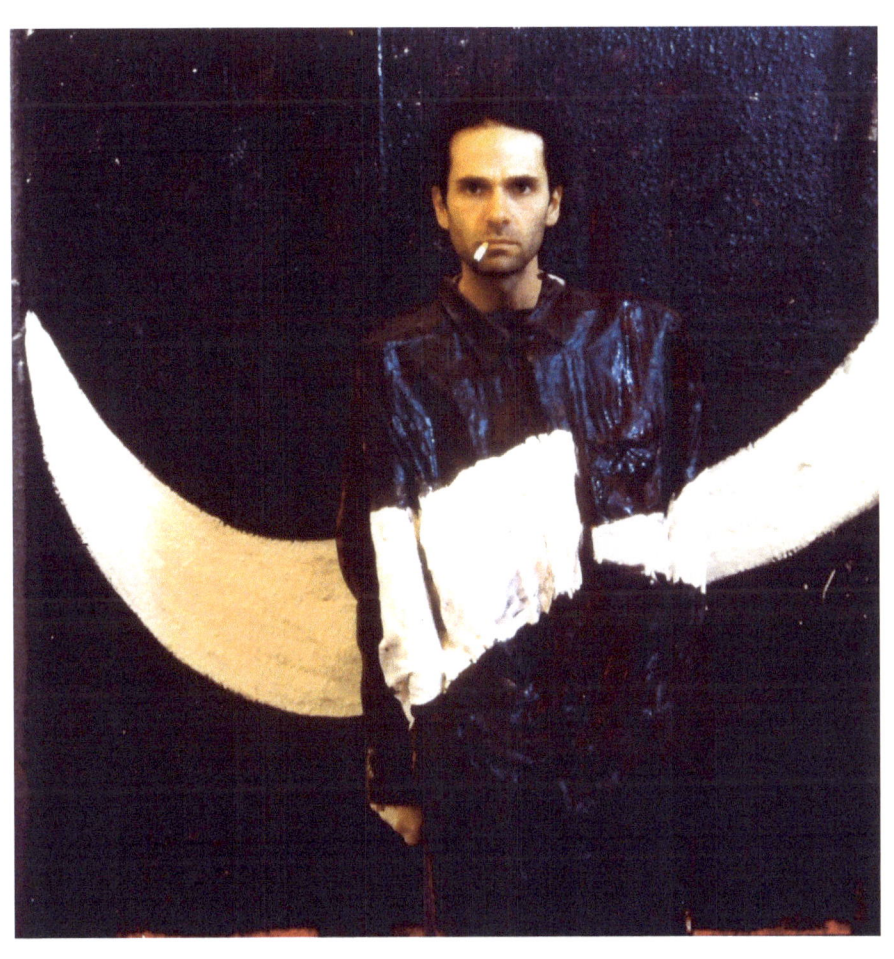

Self-portrait as Mike Kelley piece, 2002 Pro-cryptic painting (acrylic on board and protective suit) color photograph, 75 x 50 cm

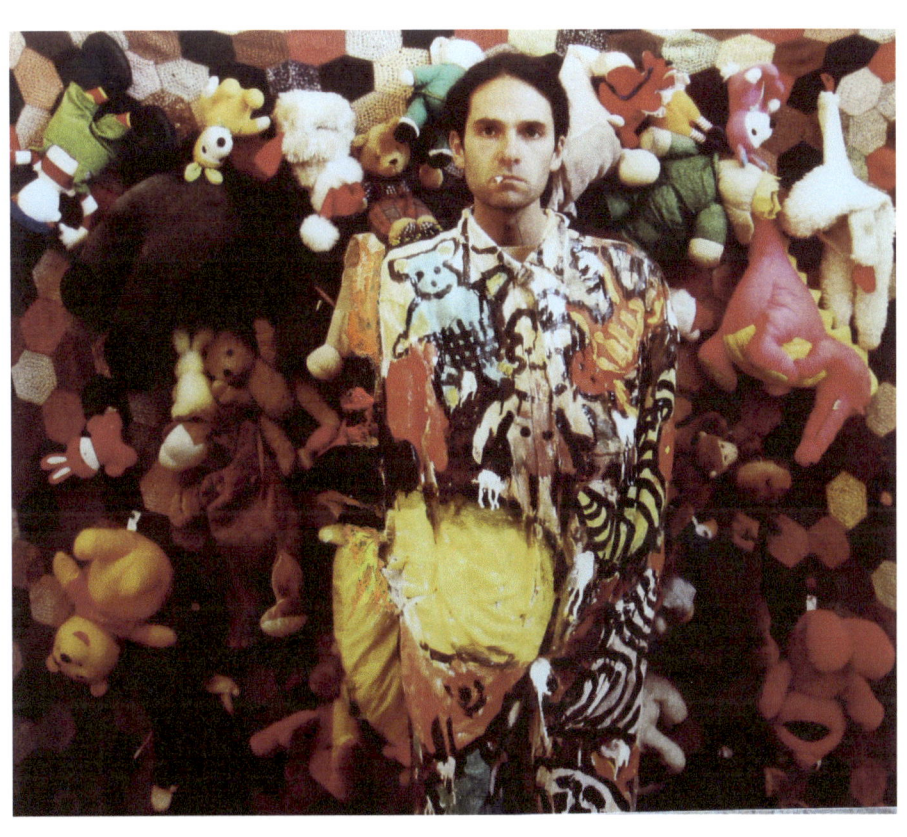

Self-portrait as Kenneth Noland's *Song*, 2002 Pro-cryptic painting (acrylic on board and protective suit) color photograph, 75 x 50 cm

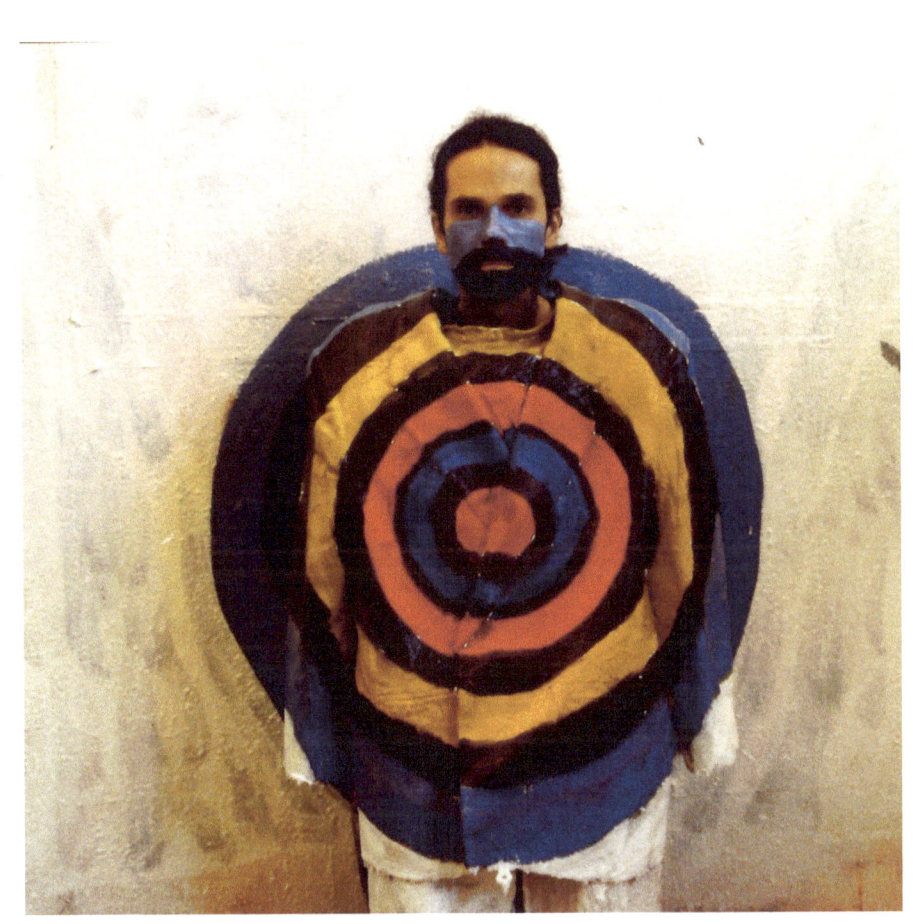

Self-portrait as Jean-Michel Basquiat's *Hollywood Africans*, 2002 Pro-cryptic painting (acrylic on board and protective suit) color photograph, 75 x 50 cm

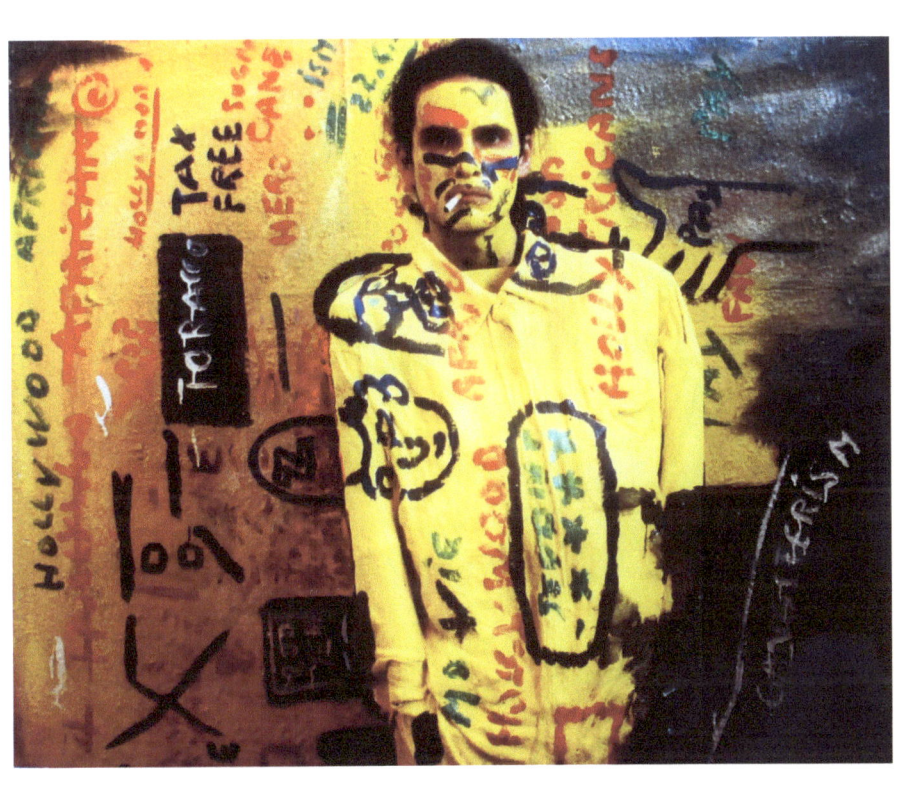

Self-portrait as Jim Dine's *A black Shovel Number* 2, 2002 Pro-cryptic painting (acrylic on board and protective suit) color photograph, 75 x 50 cm

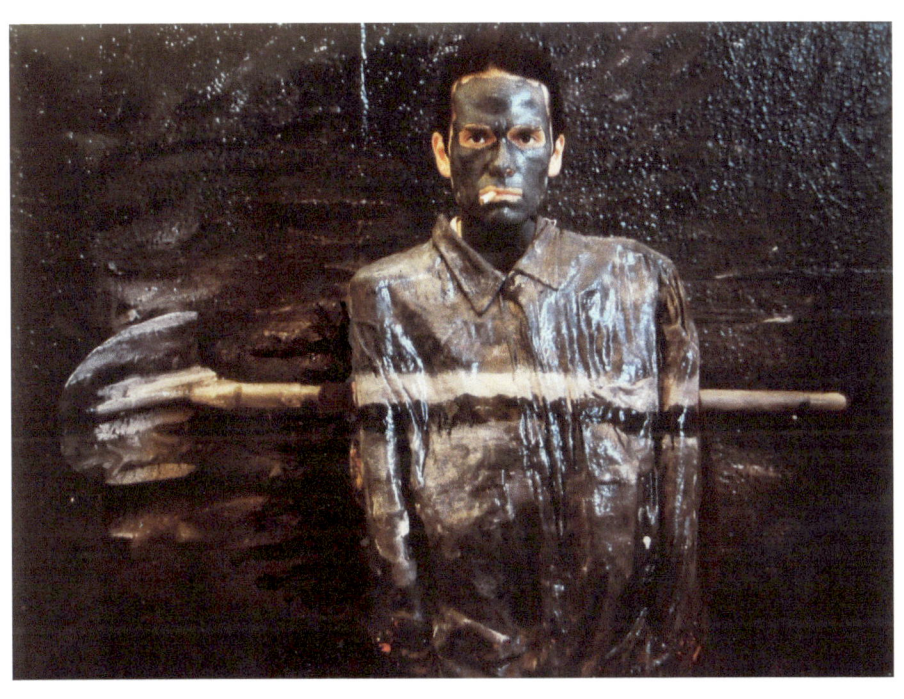

Self-portrait as Roy Lichtenstein's *In the car*, 2002
Pro-cryptic painting (acrylic on board and protective suit)
color photograph, 75 x 50 cm

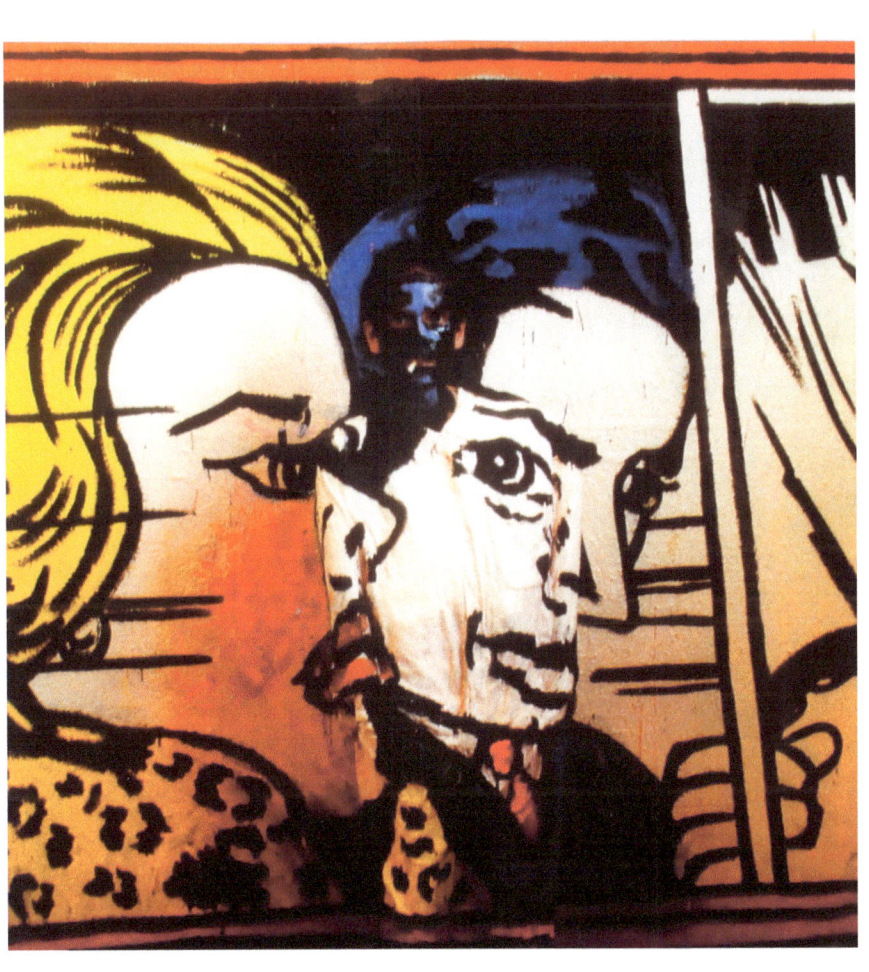

Self-portrait as a Bill Viola video installation, 2002
Pro-cryptic painting (acrylic on board and protective suit)
color photograph, 75 x 50 cm

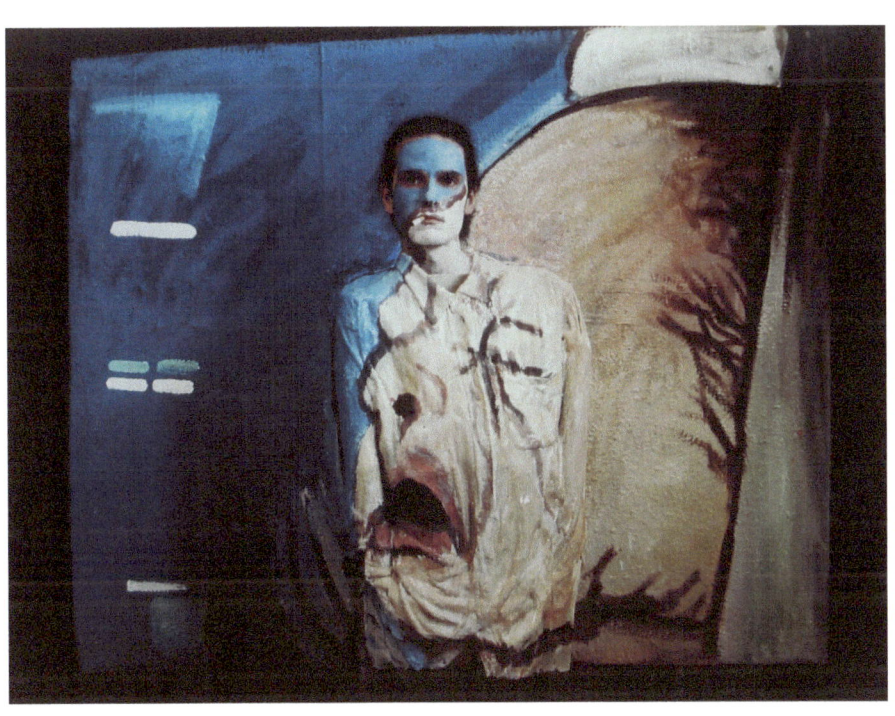

Self-portrait as Alexander Calder's *Big Red*, 2002 Pro-
cryptic painting (acrylic on board and protective suit) color
photograph, 75 x 50 cm

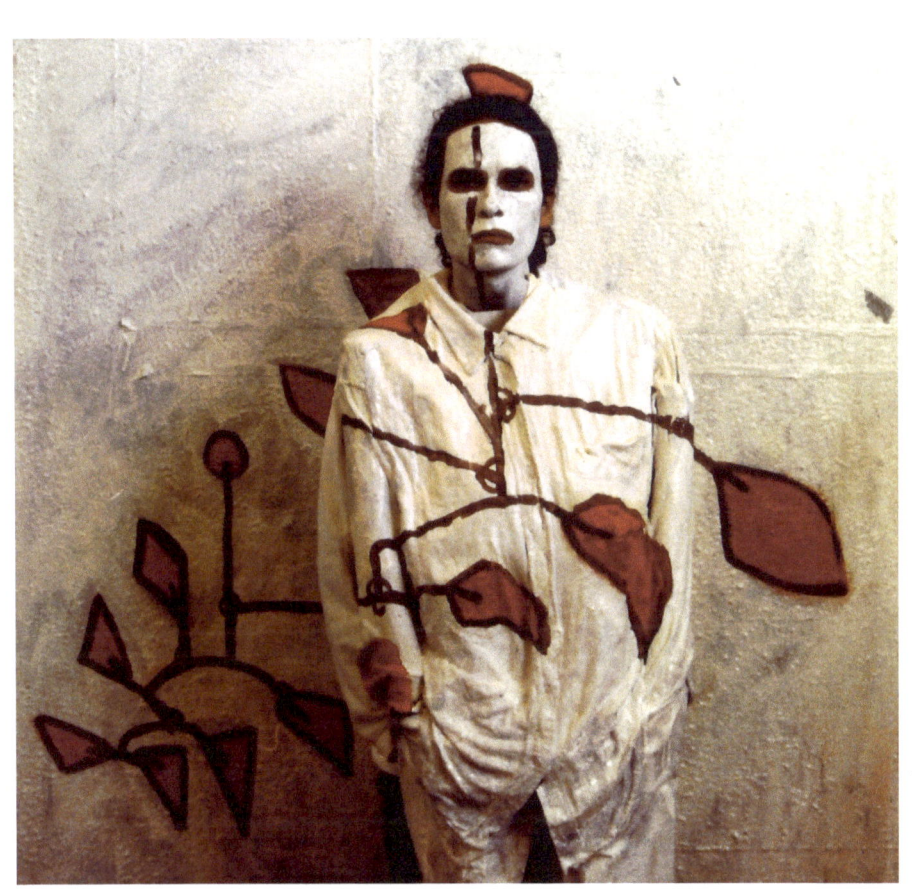

Self-portrait as Sam Francis's *Around the blues*, 2002
Pro-cryptic painting (acrylic on board and protective suit)
color photograph, 75 x 50 cm

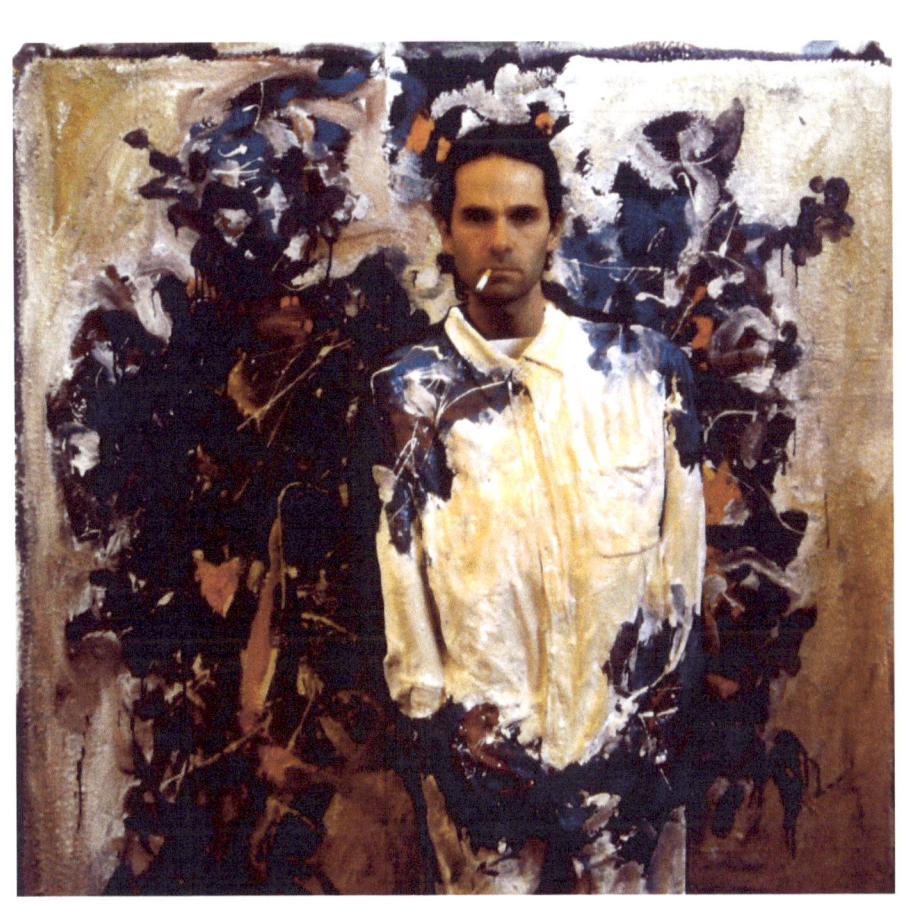

Self-portrait as Sol Le Witt's *Composition 22990*, 2002 Pro-cryptic painting (acrylic on board and protective suit) color photograph, 75 x 50 cm

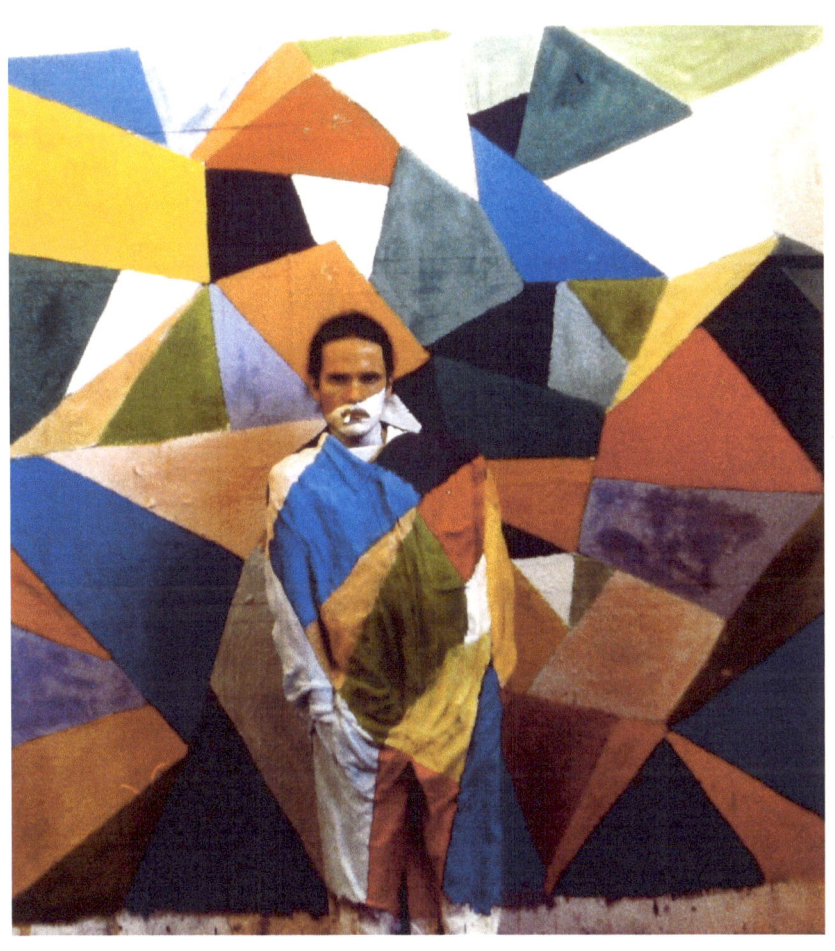

Self-portrait as Morris Louis's *Gamma Delta*, 2002
Pro-cryptic painting (acrylic on board and protective suit)
color photograph, 75 x 50 cm

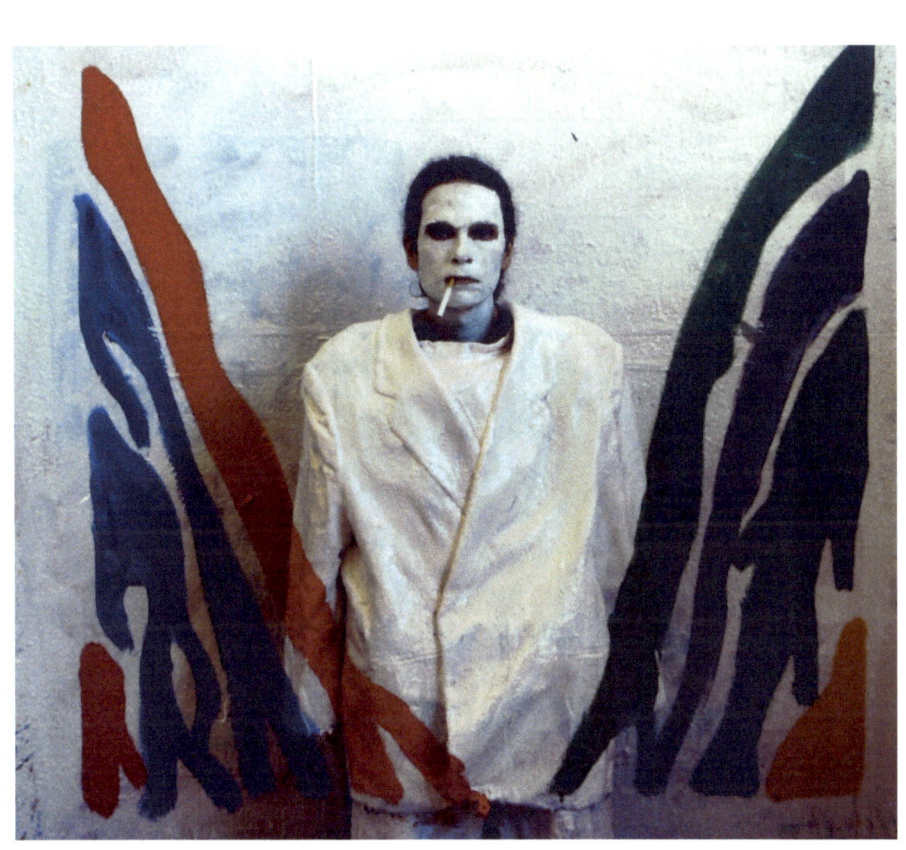

Self-portrait as Robert Mangold's *Three Red X Within X*, 2002 Pro-cryptic painting (acrylic on board and protective suit) color photograph, 75 x 50 cm

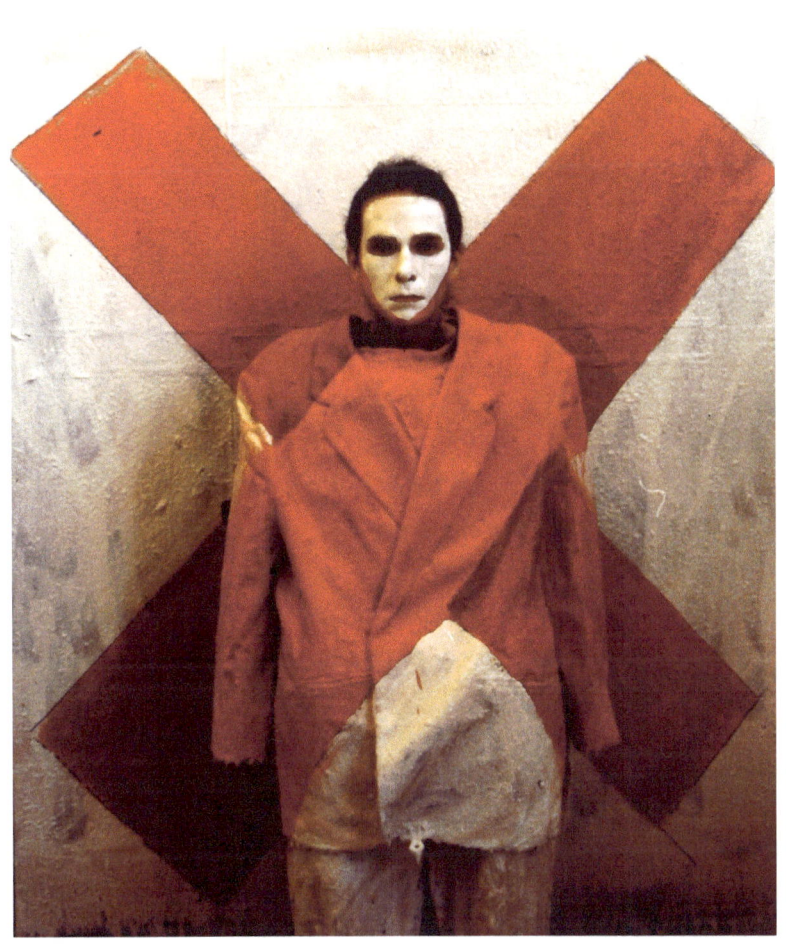

Self-portrait as Andy Warhol´s *Marilyn*, 2002 Pro-cryptic painting (acrylic on board and protective suit) color photograph, 75 x 50 cm

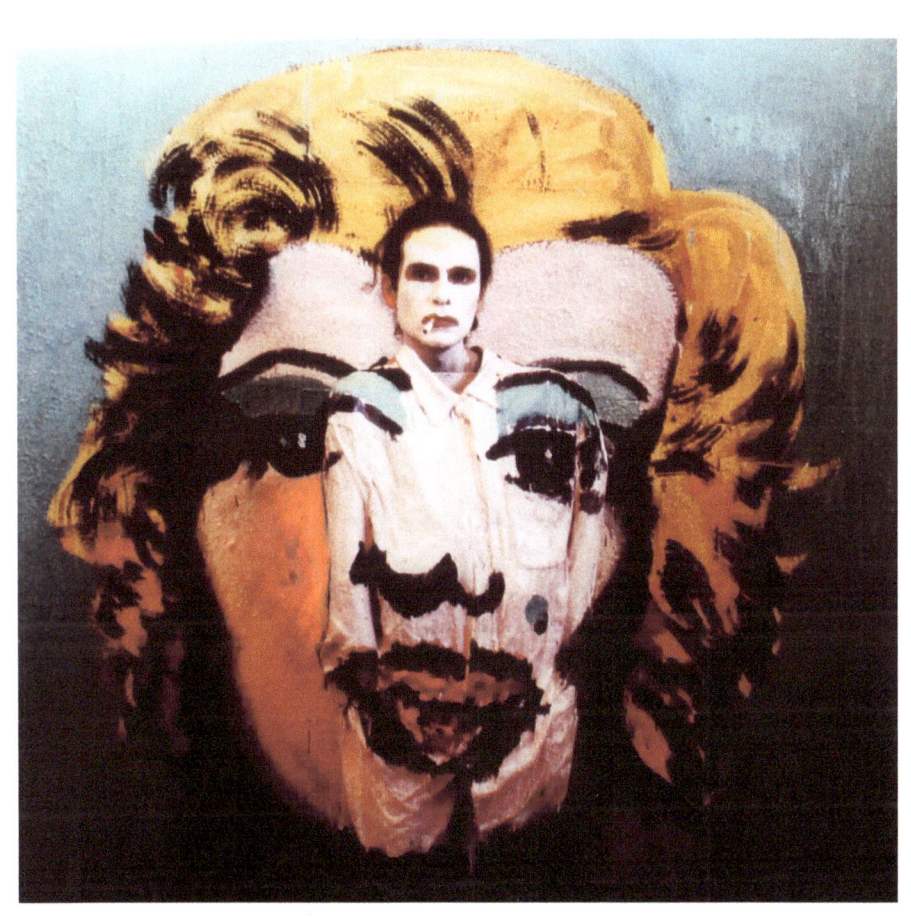

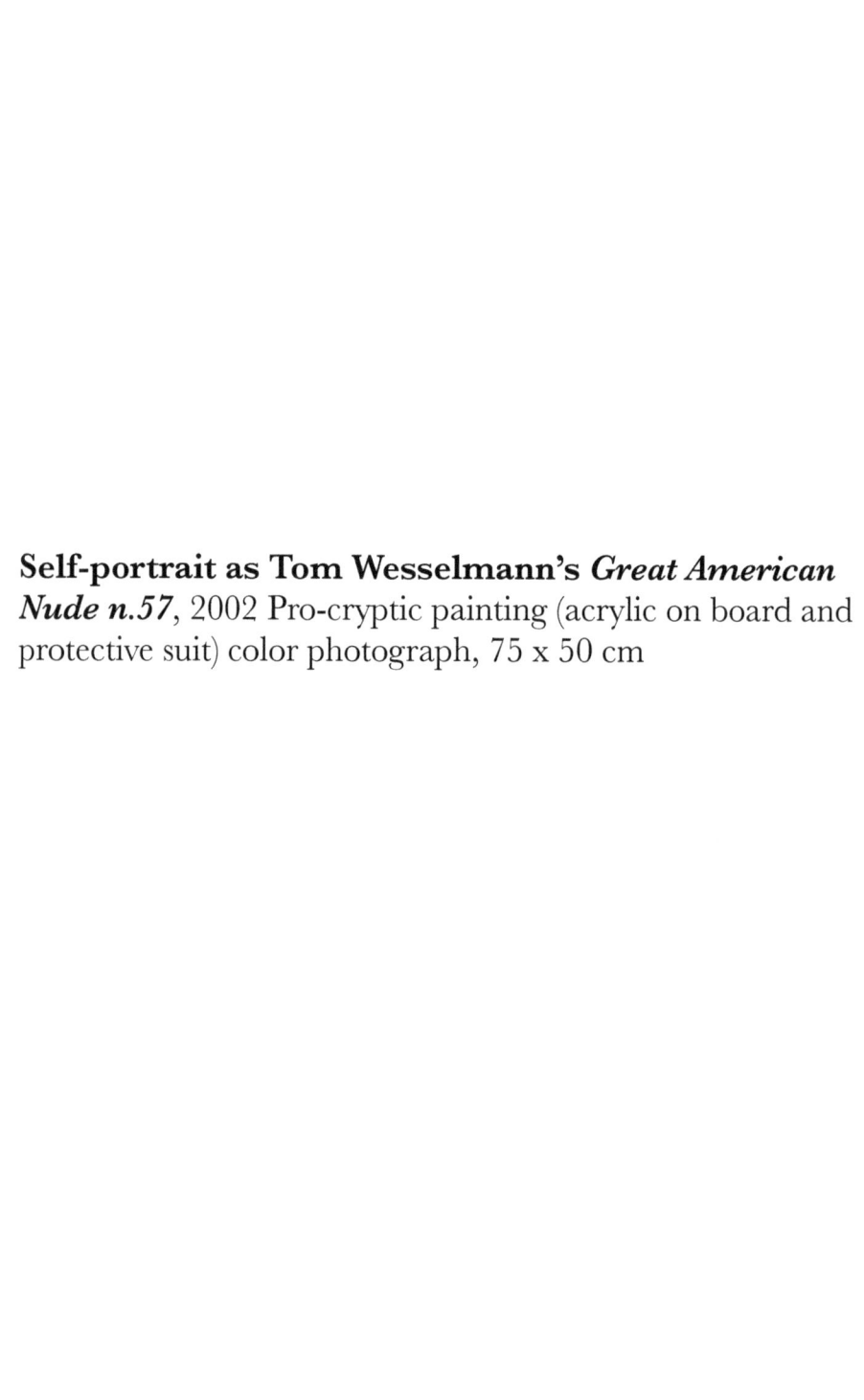

Self-portrait as Tom Wesselmann's *Great American Nude n.57*, 2002 Pro-cryptic painting (acrylic on board and protective suit) color photograph, 75 x 50 cm

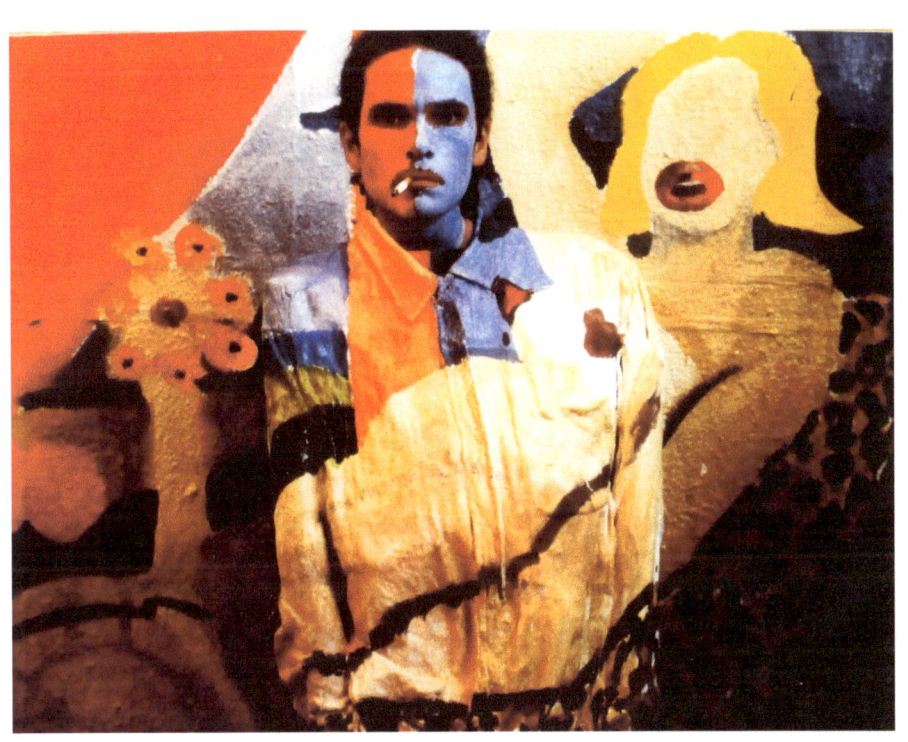

Self-portrait as Philip Guston's *Sleeping*, 2002 Pro-cryptic painting (acrylic on board and protective suit) color photograph, 75 x 50 cm

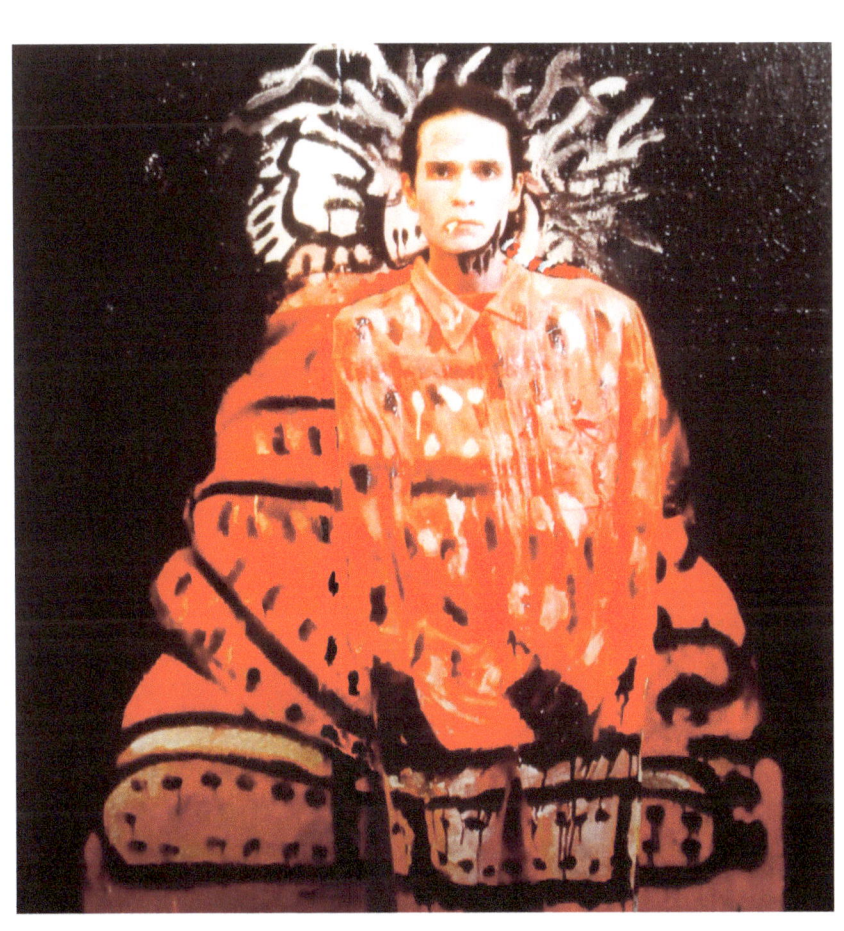

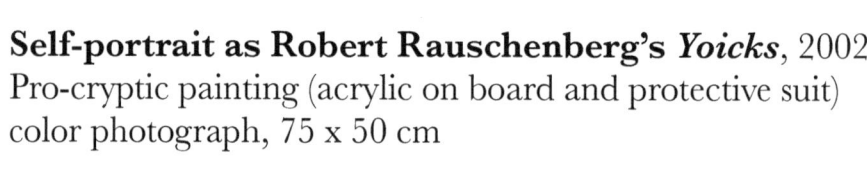

Self-portrait as Robert Rauschenberg's *Yoicks*, 2002
Pro-cryptic painting (acrylic on board and protective suit)
color photograph, 75 x 50 cm

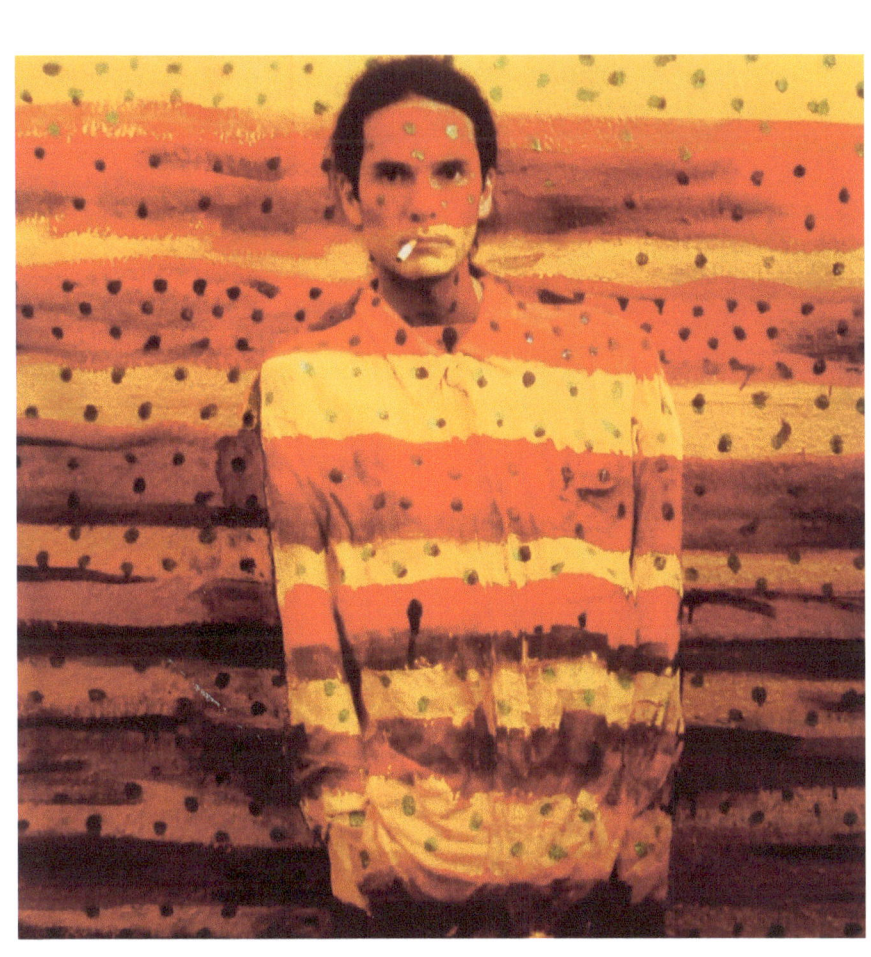

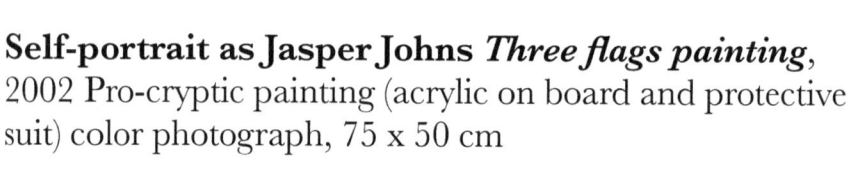

Self-portrait as Jasper Johns *Three flags painting*, 2002 Pro-cryptic painting (acrylic on board and protective suit) color photograph, 75 x 50 cm

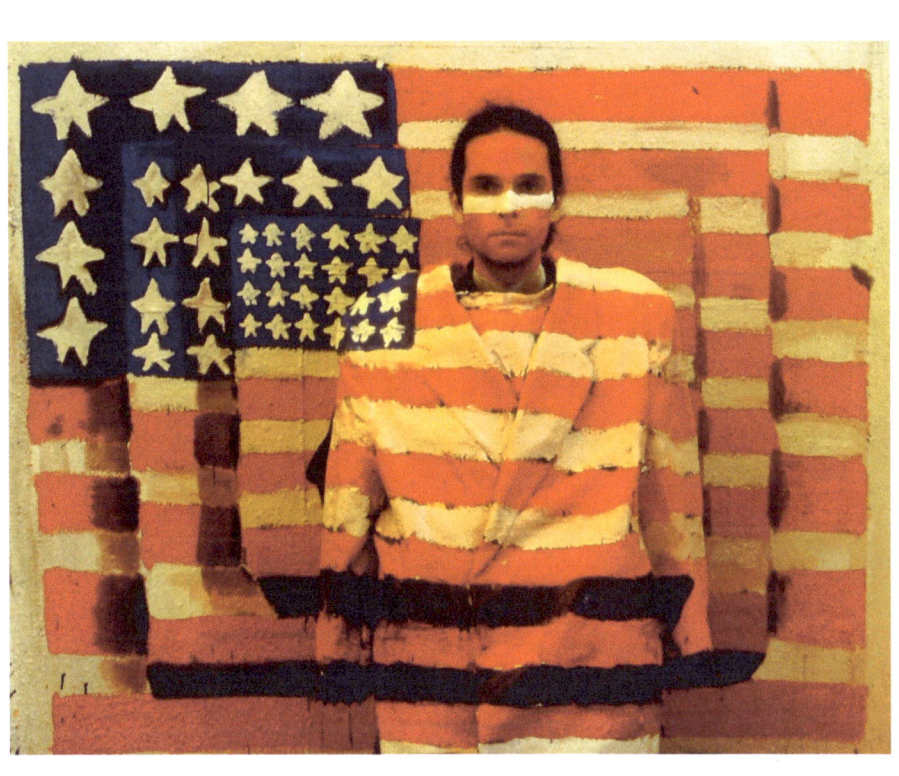

Self-portrait as Robert Mapplethorpe's *Marty and Veronica*, 2002 Pro-cryptic painting (acrylic on board and protective suit) color photograph, 75 x 50 cm

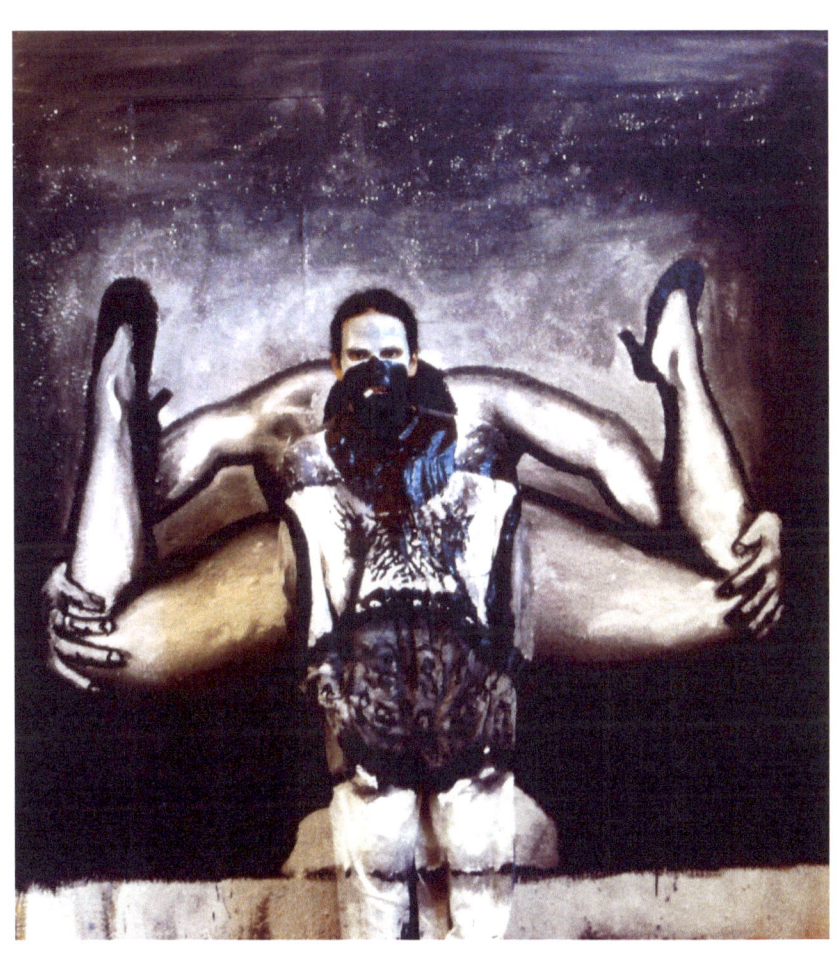

Self-portrait as a Willem de Kooning painting, 2002
Pro-cryptic painting (acrylic on board and protective suit)
color photograph, 75 x 50 cm

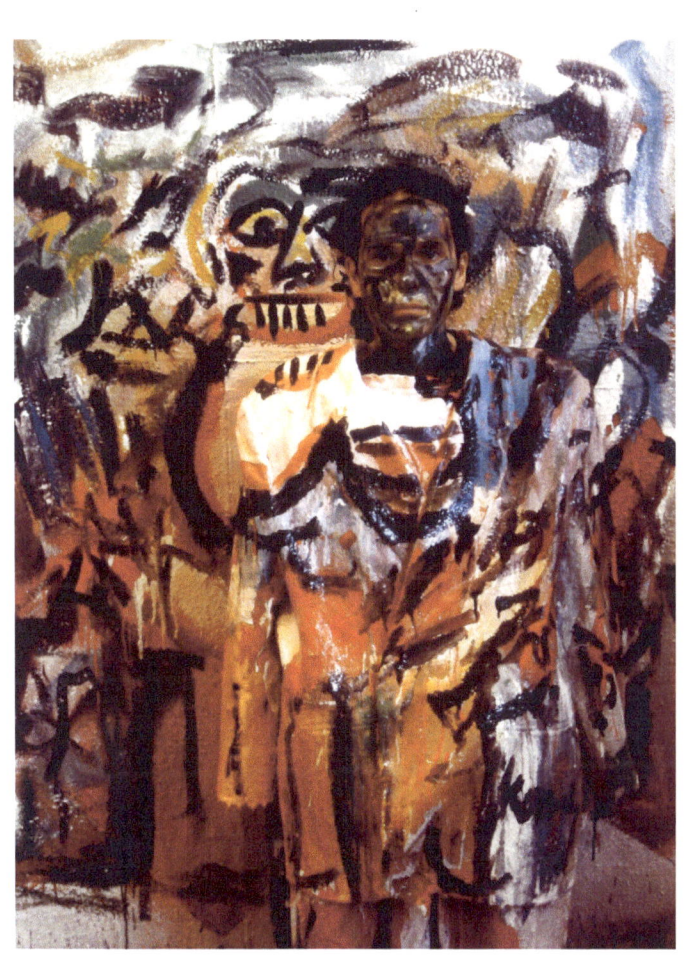

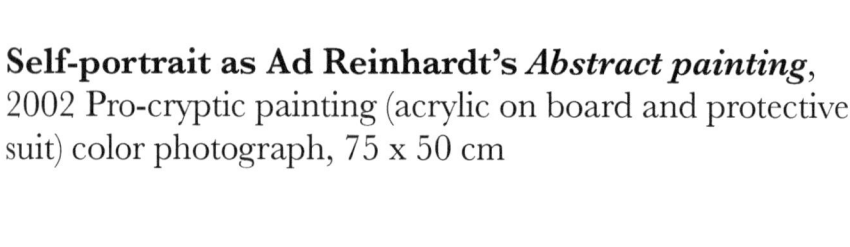

Self-portrait as Ad Reinhardt's *Abstract painting*, 2002 Pro-cryptic painting (acrylic on board and protective suit) color photograph, 75 x 50 cm

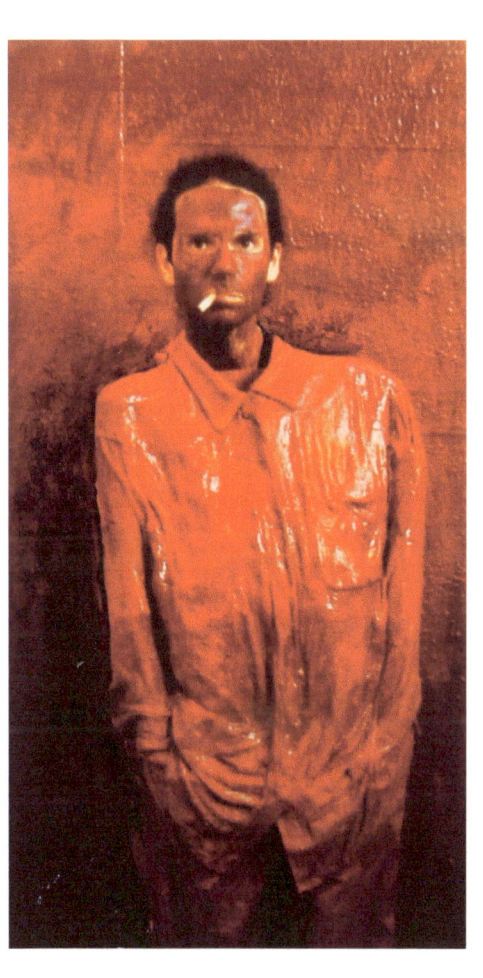

Self-portrait as Clyfford Still´s *Untitled*, 2002 Pro-cryptic painting (acrylic on board and protective suit) color photograph, 75 x 50 cm

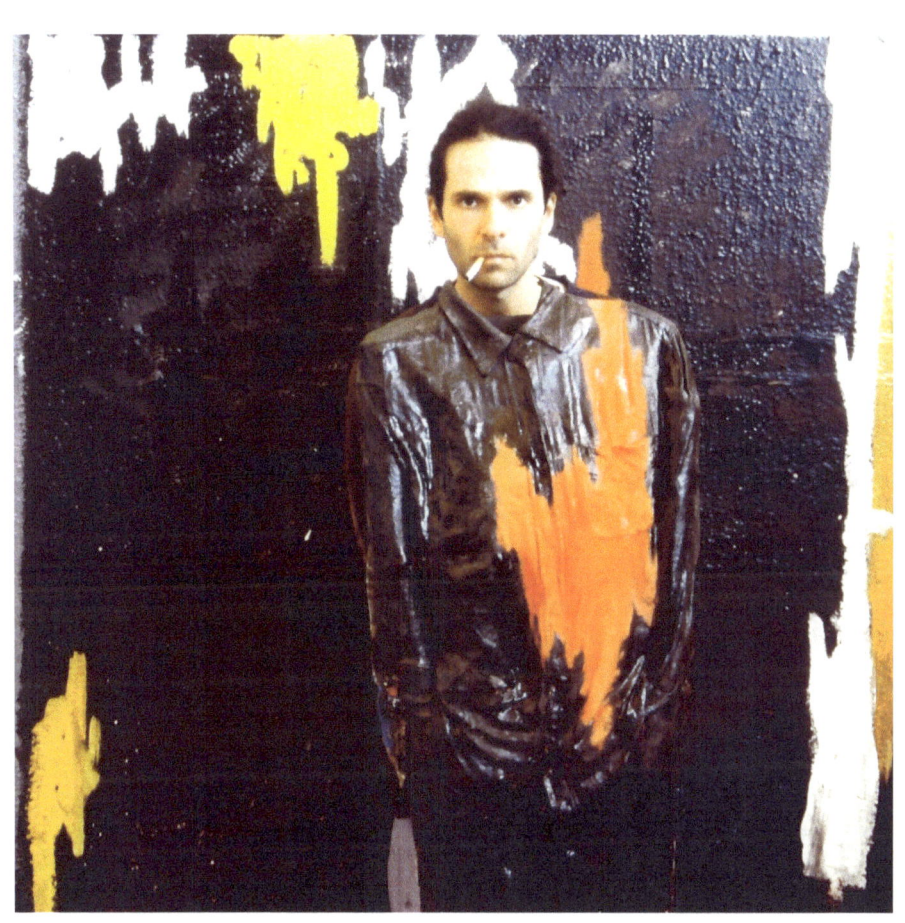

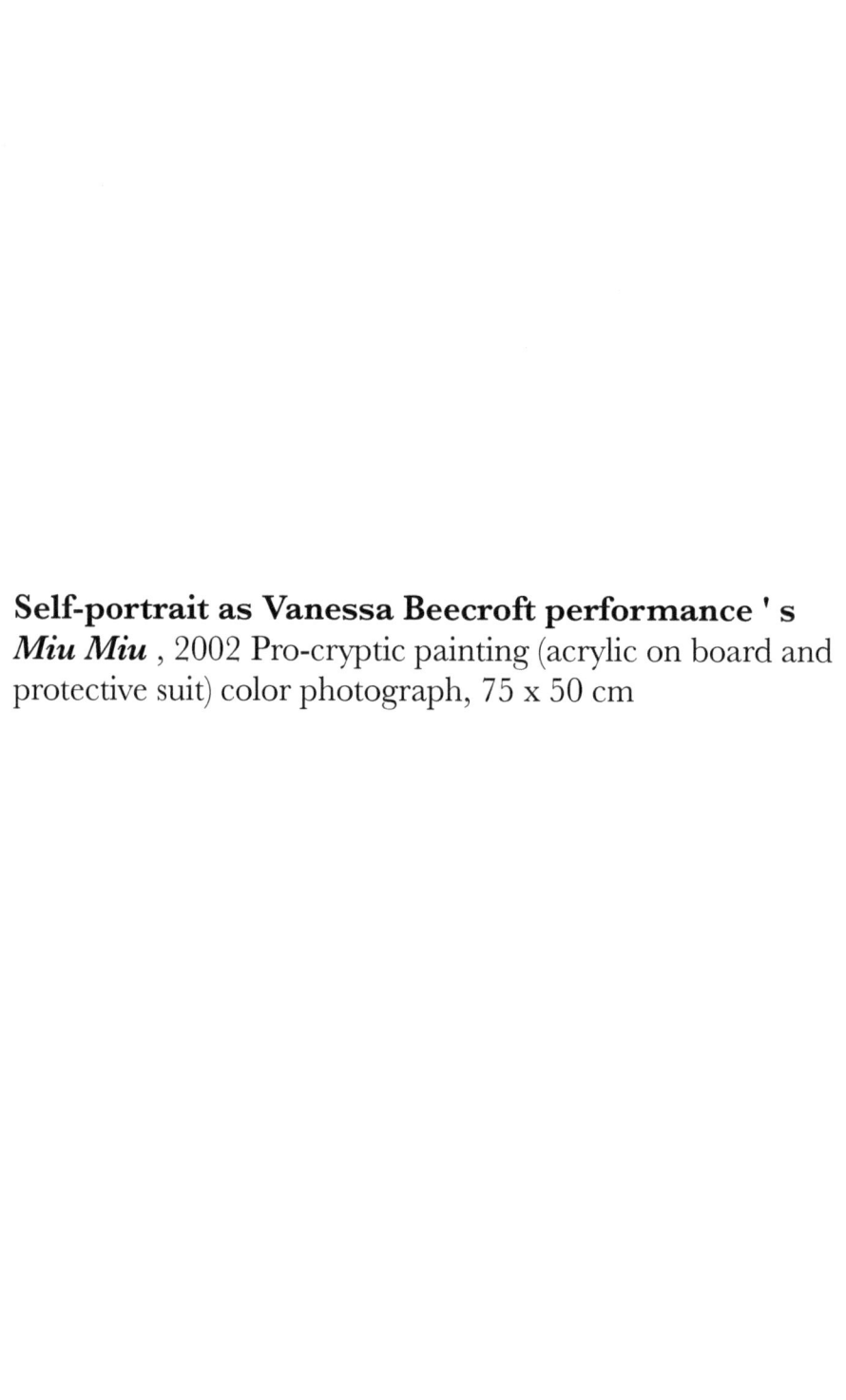

Self-portrait as Vanessa Beecroft performance ' s
Miu Miu , 2002 Pro-cryptic painting (acrylic on board and
protective suit) color photograph, 75 x 50 cm

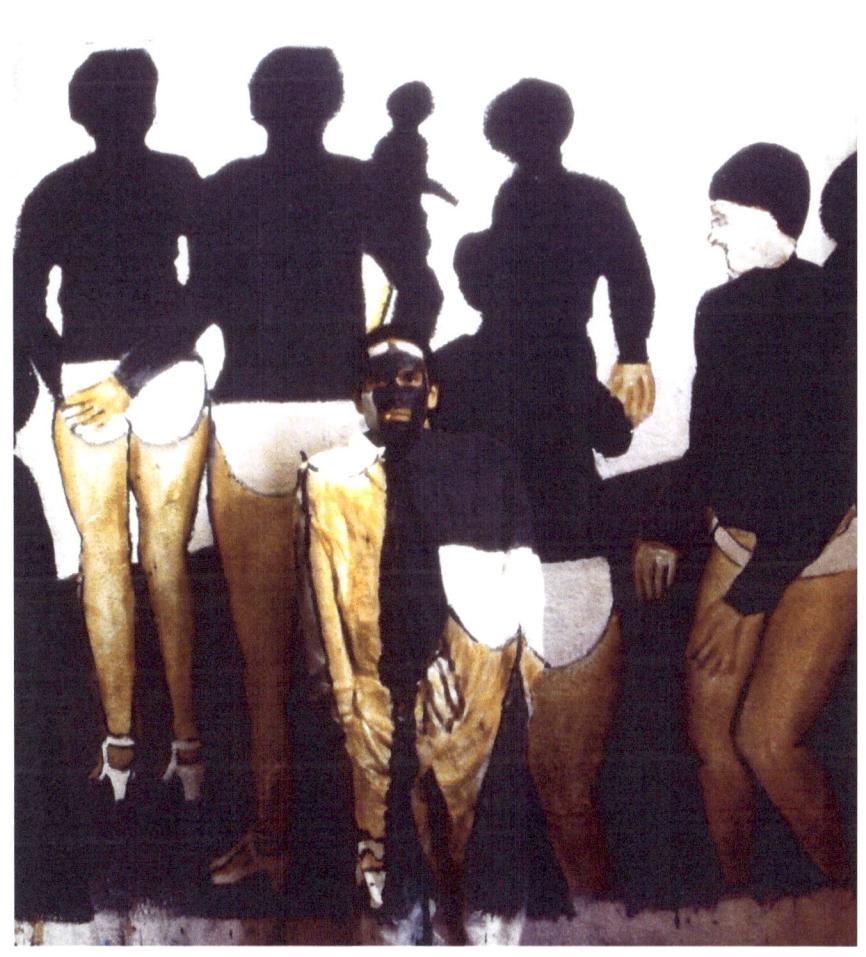

CONTENTS:

Introduction

Preface by Lyn Cole

1- **Self-portrait as a Jackson Pollock painting**, 2002 Pro-cryptic painting (acrylic on board and protective suit) color photograph, 75 x 50 cm

2- **Self-portrait as Cy Twombly's *Untitled***, 2002 Pro-cryptic painting (acrylic on board and protective suit) color photograph, 75 x 50 cm

3- **Self-portrait as Frank Stella's *Kastura*,** 2002 Pro-cryptic painting (acrylic on board and protective suit) color photograph, 75 x 50 cm

4 - **Self-portrait as Edward Hopper ´s *A woman in the sun***, 2002 Pro-cryptic painting (acrylic on board and protective suit) color photograph, 75 x 50 cm

5- **Self-portrait as Ellsworth Kelly's *Atlantic***, 2002 Pro-cryptic painting (acrylic on board and protective suit) color photograph, 75 x 50 cm

6- **Self-portrait as Mike Kelley piece**, 2002 Pro-cryptic painting (acrylic on board and protective suit) color photograph, 75 x 50 cm

7- Self-portrait as Kenneth Noland's *Song*, 2002 Pro-cryptic painting (acrylic on board and protective suit) color photograph, 75 x 50 cm

8- Self-portrait as Jean-Michel Basquiat's *Hollywood Africans*, 2002 Pro-cryptic painting (acrylic on board and protective suit) color photograph, 75 x 50 cm

9- Self-portrait as Jim Dine's *A black Shovel Number* 2, 2002 Pro-cryptic painting (acrylic on board and protective suit) color photograph, 75 x 50 cm

10- Self-portrait as Roy Lichtenstein's *In the car*, 2002 Pro-cryptic painting (acrylic on board and protective suit) color photograph, 75 x 50 cm

11- Self-portrait as a Bill Viola video installation, 2002 Pro-cryptic painting (acrylic on board and protective suit) color photograph, 75 x 50 cm

12- Self-portrait as Alexander Calder's *Big Red*, 2002 Pro-cryptic painting (acrylic on board and protective suit) color photograph, 75 x 50 cm

13- Self-portrait as Sam Francis's *Around the blues*, 2002 Pro-cryptic painting (acrylic on board and protective suit) color photograph, 75 x 50 cm

14- Self-portrait as Sol Le Witt's *Composition 22990*, 2002 Pro-cryptic painting (acrylic on board and protective suit) color photograph, 75 x 50 cm

15- **Self-portrait as Morris Louis's** *Gamma Delta*, 2002 Pro-cryptic painting (acrylic on board and protective suit) color photograph, 75 x 50 cm

16- **Self-portrait as Robert Mangold's** *Three Red X Within X*, 2002 Pro-cryptic painting (acrylic on board and protective suit) color photograph, 75 x 50 cm

17- **Self-portrait as Andy Warhol 's** *Marilyn*, 2002 Pro-cryptic painting (acrylic on board and protective suit) color photograph, 75 x 50 cm

18-**Self-portrait as Tom Wesselmann's** *Great American Nude n.57*, 2002 Pro-cryptic painting (acrylic on board and protective suit) color photograph, 75 x 50 cm

19- **Self-portrait as Philip Guston's** *Sleeping*, 2002 Pro-cryptic painting (acrylic on board and protective suit) color photograph, 75 x 50 cm

20- **Self-portrait as Robert Rauschenberg's** *Yoicks*, 2002 Pro-cryptic painting (acrylic on board and protective suit) color photograph, 75 x 50 cm

21**- Self-portrait as Jasper Johns** *Three flags painting*, 2002 Pro-cryptic painting (acrylic on board and protective suit) color photograph, 75 x 50 cm

22-**Self-portrait as Robert Mapplethorpe's** *Marty and Veronica*, 2002 Pro-cryptic painting (acrylic on board and protective suit) color photograph, 75 x 50 cm

23- **Self-portrait as a Willem de Kooning painting**, 2002 Pro-cryptic painting (acrylic on board and protective suit) color photograph, 75 x 50 cm

24- **Self-portrait as Ad Reinhardt's *Abstract painting***, 2002 Pro-cryptic painting (acrylic on board and protective suit) color photograph, 75 x 50 cm

25- **Self-portrait as Clyfford Still ´s *Untitled***, 2002 Pro-cryptic painting (acrylic on board and protective suit) color photograph, 75 x 50 cm

26- **Self-portrait as Vanessa Beecroft performance ´s *Miu Miu***, 2002 Pro-cryptic painting (acrylic on board and protective suit) color photograph, 75 x 50 cm

About the artist

Laurent La Gamba was born on January 23rd, 1967, in Bondy, France.

After studying at the Sorbonne in Paris he travels abroad, staying for long periods of time in Los Angeles, California, in the United States. There his painting evolves hand in hand with photography.

On his return to France he begins the first in situ series of camouflages and pro-cryptic installations (2001). He is working on these when he obtains a Pollock-Krasner Foundation grant and becomes artist-in-residence at La Napoule Art Foundation in Mandelieu. His work tilts into conceptual photography at this point.

While exploring the meaning of camouflage he creates painted installations for his static effigy. He dresses his models or himself in white suits which are then painted into a chosen environment so that they disappear. At first there are indoor portraits and then more elaborate outdoor portraits i.e. camouflage in supermarkets, airports, in front of cars, refrigerators, cookers etc.

Trained as a painter, Laurent La Gamba's photographs also rely on the aspect of performance.

Excerpts from psychoanalyst Jacques Lacan's writings often accompany the artist's work.

Laurent La Gamba

A *Contribution to American Art History*,

26 revisited works from the Whitney Museum
(Preface by Lyn Cole)

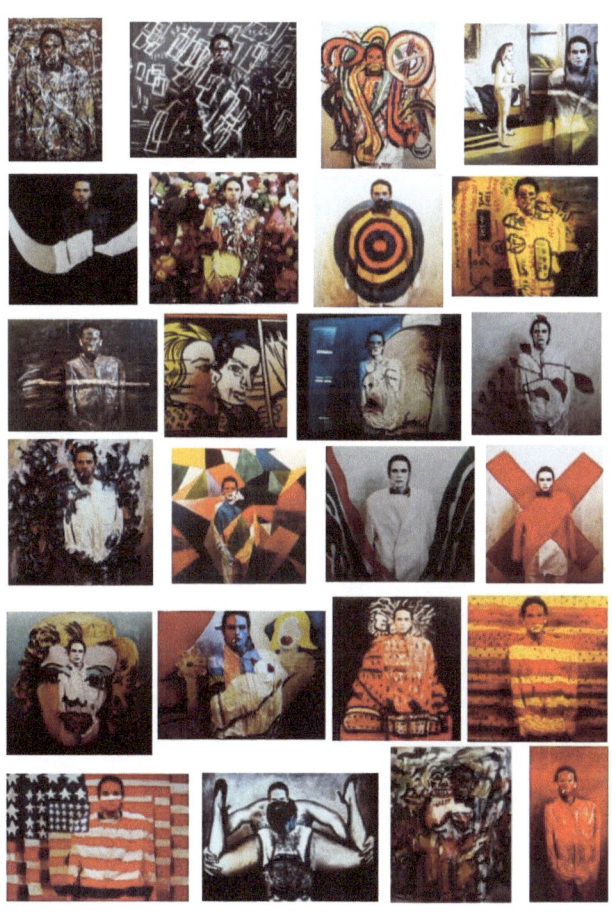

Matisse 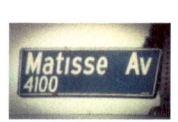 Avenue Books

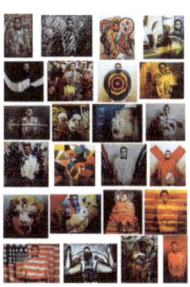

Laurent La Gamba
A Contribution to American Art History,
26 revisited works from the Whitney Museum.

ISBN: 9781500568290

Printed in the United States of America

Matisse 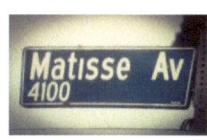 *Avenue Books*

www.ingramcontent.com/pod-product-compliance
Lightning Source LLC
Chambersburg PA
CBHW040835180526
45159CB00001B/197